Friends of the
Houston Public Library

SCIENCE DETECTIVES

Investigating Volcanic Eruptions

Ellen René

PowerKiDS press
New York

To Harvey, forever and always

Published in 2009 by The Rosen Publishing Group, Inc.
29 East 21st Street, New York, NY 10010

Copyright © 2009 by The Rosen Publishing Group, Inc.

All rights reserved. No part of this book may be reproduced in any form without permission in writing from the publisher, except by a reviewer.

First Edition

Editor: Joanne Randolph
Book Design: Julio Gil
Photo Researcher: Jessica Gerweck

Photo Credits: Cover, back cover (top center, top right, middle left, bottom left), pp. 6, 17, 21 Shutterstock.com; back cover, (middle center) © Jim Merli; back cover, (middle right) © Fat Chance Productions; pp. 5, 10, 14 © Getty Images; p. 9 © Photodisc; p. 13 © National Geographic/Getty Images; p. 18 © AFP/Getty Images.

Library of Congress Cataloging-in-Publication Data

René, Ellen.
  Investigating volcanic eruptions / Ellen René.
       p. cm. — (Science detectives)
  Includes index.
  ISBN 978-1-4042-4481-8 (library binding)
  1. Volcanoes—Juvenile literature. 2. Volcanism—Juvenile literature. I. Title.
  QE521.3.R46 2009
  551.21—dc22
                                          2007051955

Manufactured in the United States of America

Contents

A Sleeping Giant Wakes   4
What Are Volcanoes?   7
From Core to Crust   8
What Is Going on Under There?   11
The Magma Chamber   12
Where Will All the Magma Go?   15
She's Going to Blow!   16
Asking the Right Questions   19
What Happens Next?   20
Predicting Volcanic Eruptions   22
Glossary   23
Index   24
Web Sites   24

A Sleeping Giant Wakes

In 1980, scientists watched and waited. A sleeping volcano named Mount St. Helens, in Washington, roared awake. **Earthquakes** and explosions shook the mountain. It **cracked**. It swelled. Gas poured out. A huge bump formed on the north side. What was happening? Scientists looked for clues. They measured the growing bulge and the strength of the quakes. The results worried them. Would the volcano **erupt**, and if so, when?

On May 18, 1980, Mount St. Helens erupted. The bulge tore loose and crashed down the mountain. Hot gases, broken rock, and ice blasted out the mountain's side. **Ash** clouds made the day dark as night.

Here Mount St. Helens is letting off steam. It is still an active volcano and has had another eruption since the large one in 1980.

Here red-hot lava flows from a volcano.
Some people call volcanoes fire fountains.

What Are Volcanoes?

Mount St. Helens is just one of thousands of volcanoes around the world. Many people spend their lives studying volcanoes and trying to guess when they will erupt. What exactly is a volcano, though? Volcanoes are openings in Earth where melted rock, hot gases, and ash come out. Right now, about 20 volcanoes are erupting around the world. Some explode. Others quietly ooze hot, liquid rock called lava.

All volcanoes do not look or act alike. Their size, shape, and eruptions have to do with the forces creating them. Let's investigate how volcanoes work.

Volcanoes that have explosive eruptions usually have gentle hills toward the bottom and steeper sides toward the top. Volcanoes that have quieter eruptions and thinner lava have a wider, flatter shape with gentle slopes, or sides that are not that steep.

From Core to Crust

Earth's mantle holds almost all Earth's minerals, which are the building blocks of rocks. Even though it is mostly solid, or hard, the mantle flows like warm taffy.

To understand volcanoes, we need to know a little bit about Earth. Pretend you could cut Earth in half like a hard-boiled egg. In the center, you would see the **core**, like the egg's yolk. Outside that, you would see Earth's middle part, or mantle, like the white part of the egg. Around all this is Earth's **crust**, which is like the eggshell.

We live on Earth's thin crust. The crust is broken into giant pieces. Like cracked ice on a pond, these pieces float on top of the mantle. The mantle is made up of super hot rock and **magma**.

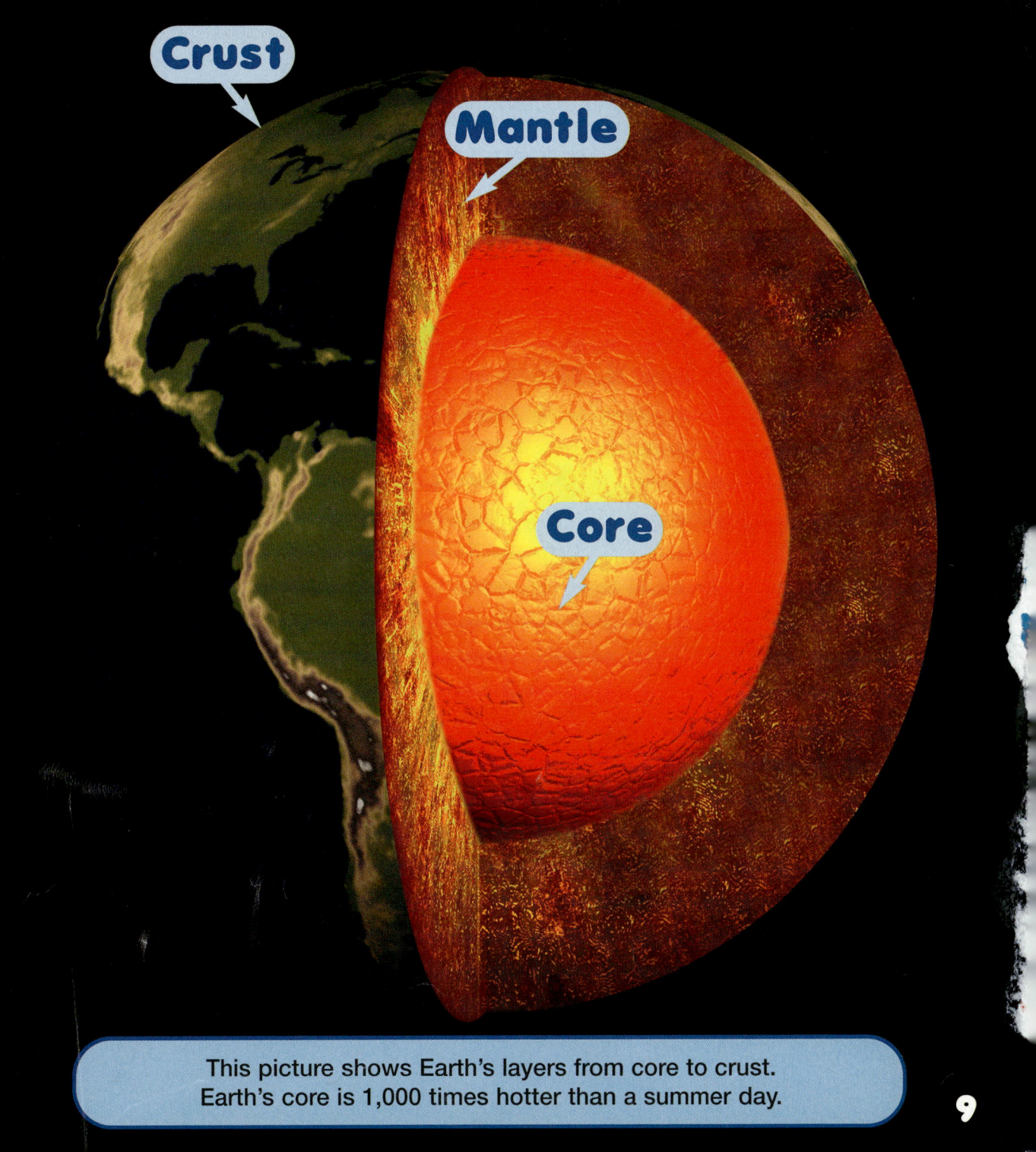

This picture shows Earth's layers from core to crust. Earth's core is 1,000 times hotter than a summer day.

Lava is made of hot melted rock. The lava will cool on Earth's surface and become rock.

What Is Going on Under There?

The floating pieces of Earth's crust are called plates. They travel about 2 inches (5 cm) a year. Most volcanoes are found near plate edges.

When plates move apart, this can cause cracks in Earth's surface. Hot magma from the mantle rises out through these cracks. Magma is called lava once it is on the surface.

When plates come together, one can slide under the other. An edge is pushed down into the mantle. That part of the plate melts, forming magma. This magma rises to the surface as lava during an eruption.

Some volcanoes form over hot spots. Hot spots are places away from plate edges where burning magma is close to the surface. One of the best known hot spots is in the Pacific Ocean. It formed all the Hawaiian islands.

The Magma Chamber

Different kinds of rocks and minerals make different kinds of magma. Some rocks make fast-moving magma that explodes with great force and flows quickly. Other rocks make slow-moving magma.

If we were looking for the place where the volcano gets its start, where should we look? We need to look for a place that is hot enough and has high enough **pressure** to melt rock. The mantle is just the place for both of these things. A volcano gets its start deep inside the mantle, where the heat and pressure have formed magma. If we follow the magma, we may find a volcano.

Lighter than the rock around it, magma rises. Near the surface, it forms pools, called magma chambers. Inside the chamber, magma bubbles and mixes.

This slow-moving lava is covered by black ash. Some lava moves so slowly it hardens before it moves away from the volcano's opening.

Here steam rises from Mount St. Helens's lava dome. Steam can tell scientists something about what is going on inside the volcano.

Where Will All the Magma Go?

As more magma flows into the chamber, pressure builds. Think about what happens when you blow up a balloon. At some point, there is no room for more air. If you keep pushing more air in anyway, the balloon will pop.

This is what happens when more and more magma enters the magma chamber, too. The magma needs somewhere to go. It rises from the chamber and tries to find a way out. The slopes of the volcano above it might swell. Cracks might appear. Scientists studying volcanoes look for these kinds of changes. They help **predict** eruptions.

It is not as hot close to Earth's crust as it is deeper inside Earth. Molten rock inside a magma chamber is still very hot, though. It can reach 2,192° F (1,200° C). That is about 10 times hotter than boiling water.

She's Going to Blow!

When pressures inside magma chambers get too great, magma shoots out. Like toothpaste squeezed from a tube, it pushes up through cracks or openings to the surface.

Magma contains gases. Some can hurt living things. Some stink like rotten eggs. As the magma rises, this gas gets bigger. If the gas can escape the magma easily, there is usually a quiet eruption. Sometimes there is a lot of gas in the magma or the gas gets trapped in the magma. When this kind of magma erupts and the gas gets free, it explodes from the volcano with great force.

Trapped gases explode from the opening in this volcano and send lava shooting into the air.

The Piton de la Fournaise volcano is found on the French island of Reunion. This volcano has thin, fast-moving lava.

Asking the Right Questions

Volcanoes erupt in different ways. Scientists ask many questions that will help them guess how a volcano may erupt. Did water mix with the magma? This can make for very powerful explosions. Is there a little or a lot of gas in the molten magma and lava? Is the lava thick and runny or stiff and sticky? The answer to these questions means the difference between a quiet and a **violent** eruption.

Mount St. Helens erupted stiff, thick lava and had a violent explosion. The slow-moving lava cooled before it could flow down the mountainside. It formed a **lava dome**.

What Happens Next?

Between 2004 and 2006, Mount St. Helens erupted and built a new lava dome, which is higher than the Empire State Building. The lave dome is about 1,300 feet (396 m) tall.

What happens after lava erupts from the volcano? The lava cools and hardens to form rock. This means that over time volcanoes build themselves. Lava, rock, and ash from each eruption mound up around vents, or openings in the crust.

In 1943, a volcano erupted in a Mexican cornfield. It grew 1,100 feet (335 m) in a year. Most volcanoes grow slowly. Mount St. Helens is a young volcano. It is about 40,000 years old. It stands at 8,365 feet (2,550 m), after losing 1,314 feet (400.5 m) in the 1980 eruption.

Many volcanoes form under the sea. Some of them become tall enough to rise above the sea and form islands.

Volcanoes under the Pacific Ocean made the Hawaiian Islands. This is Hawaii's Kilauea Volcano, one of the world's most active volcanoes.

Predicting Volcanic Eruptions

Volcanoes are born, erupt, sleep, wake up, and die. They destroy and kill. In A.D. 79, Mount Vesuvius wiped out two Roman towns and killed more than 3,000 people. It still is unsafe. Volcanoes also build, though. They form new land and make **fertile** soil.

Scientists are getting better at predicting when and how volcanoes will erupt. In 1980, scientists used meters on the ground to measure Mount St. Helens's growing bulge. Today **satellites** circling Earth help gather clues.

Can we tame volcanoes? Will we ever be able to use their power? There will always be questions about volcanoes. Come up with some of your own and find out the answers.

Glossary

ash (ASH) Pieces of tiny rock that shoot out of a volcano when it blows.

core (KOR) The hot center of Earth that is made of liquid rock.

cracked (KRAKT) Broke open or apart.

crust (KRUST) The outside of a planet, such as Earth.

earthquakes (URTH-kwayks) Shakings of Earth caused by the movements of large pieces of land called plates that run into or rub past each other.

erupt (ih-RUPT) To break open or have had a volcano send up gases, smoke, or lava.

fertile (FER-tul) Good for making and growing things.

lava dome (LAH-vuh DOHM) Lava that has cooled in a dome-shaped pile.

magma (MAG-muh) A hot liquid rock underneath Earth's surface.

predict (prih-DIKT) To make a guess based on facts or knowledge.

pressure (PREH-shur) A force that pushes on something.

satellites (SA-tih-lyts) Spacecraft that circle Earth.

violent (VY-lent) Strong and forceful.

Index

A
ash, 4, 7, 20

C
core, 8
crust, 8, 20

L
lava, 7, 11, 19–20
lava dome, 19

M
magma, 8, 11–12, 15–16, 19
mantle, 8, 11–12
Mount St. Helens, 4, 7, 19–20, 22
Mount Vesuvius, 22

P
plate(s), 11
pressure(s), 12, 15, 16

S
satellites, 22
scientists, 4, 15, 19, 22
soil, 22

V
vents, 20

W
Washington, 4

Web Sites

Due to the changing nature of Internet links, PowerKids Press has developed an online list of Web sites related to the subject of this book. This site is updated regularly. Please use this link to access the list:
www.powerkidslinks.com/scidet/volcan/